Picturing a Nation

THE GREAT DEPRESSION'S FINEST PHOTOGRAPHERS
INTRODUCE AMERICA TO ITSELF

MARTIN W. SANDLER

CANDLEWICK PRESS

For Anika, Omyra, and Beatrix

Our hopes rest with you

First edition 2021

Library of Congress Catalog Card Number pending
ISBN 978-1-5362-1525-0

21 22 23 24 25 26 APS 10 9 8 7 6 5 4 3 2 1

Printed in Humen, Dongguan, China

This book was typeset in Archer.

Candlewick Press
99 Dover Street
Somerville, Massachusetts 02144

www.candlewick.com

A JUNIOR LIBRARY GUILD SELECTION

CONTENTS

An Extraordinary Time

———⟩———⟨———

THE YEAR WAS 1935, and the United States was in the midst of the greatest economic depression it had ever experienced. The nation had weathered other economic crises in the past, but none had brought the country down as low as this one, known as the Great Depression.

There were several causes for the financial disaster, a number of which are still debated today. What is certain is that the crisis began in 1929 when the American stock market collapsed, brought about by huge investments in stocks that were highly overvalued. The stock market crash had a devastating spiral effect. One after another, banks that had invested heavily in stocks failed. By 1933, more than six thousand banks had closed down, leaving millions of Americans without their life savings. More than ninety thousand businesses throughout the country also failed, resulting in millions of people becoming unemployed.

The Great Depression would have been devastating enough had it been confined to the industrial and urban cities of America. But the nation's farmers, the backbone of the country, were particularly hard-hit by the financial crisis. And as if that were not disastrous enough, Mother Nature dealt a bitter blow. Farmers in the middle of the United States from the Canadian border to Texas, including a vast area of the Great Plains, were stricken by the most severe and prolonged period of drought the nation had ever experienced. The lack of rain combined with overplowing, which had stripped away the topsoil, resulted in soil that turned to dust. When huger than normal prairie winds blew across the farmland, tons of dry earth was carried aloft, destroying crops and turning an enormous portion of the country into a gigantic unplantable dust bowl.

In 1933, as the full brunt of the Great Depression was being felt, Franklin Delano Roosevelt became President of the United States. Destined to serve as chief executive longer than any other

president in the nation's history, Roosevelt, despite a privileged upbringing, had a deep sense of commitment to public service. In the first one hundred days after taking office, he created several agencies and introduced new laws designed to bring relief to Depression-crippled Americans.

One of these agencies, established in May 1935, was named the Resettlement Administration (RA). Its main purpose was to support families about to lose their farms by supporting their resettlement in rural communities or government-sponsored communal farms with low-interest loans, temporary use of farm machinery, and free distribution of government-purchased seed. To head the RA, the Roosevelt administration chose Rexford "Rex" Tugwell, a Columbia University economics professor who, since 1934, had been serving as both undersecretary of agriculture and as a close adviser to President Roosevelt. Tugwell made two important decisions. The first was to create a Historical Section within the RA, staffed with a team of photographers who would document the ways the RA was helping distressed farmers. The photographs would be used to help the agency obtain the major funding and refunding it would need from Congress. Tugwell's other key decision was to appoint a friend and longtime Columbia University colleague named Roy Stryker to serve as director of the Historical Section.

Stryker would play a major role in helping to secure funds from Congress. But at the time, no one could have envisioned the vital role he would also play in the history of photography. Certainly, no one could ever have imagined that his appointment would lead to what is widely regarded as the largest, most captivating and compassionate photographic collection ever compiled.

Stryker was not a photographer, but he had worked on documentary photography projects before. He was a firm believer in the power of pictures to record and explain what was taking place before the camera. He also had empathy for the people he was going to send his photographers out to capture on film. And he was aware that relatively few people in the country had the slightest notion about the plight of millions of rural farmers.

Stryker took great inspiration from the work of Lewis Hine, arguably the world's first great documentary photographer, who had exposed child labor in America. "There are two things I wanted to do," Hine had declared. "I wanted to show the things that had to be corrected; I wanted to show the things that had to be appreciated."

Stryker was able to take advantage of the unfortunate fact that the nation's best photographers were out of work when he was assembling his team. As the RA began, and as it was expanded and renamed the Farm Security Administration (FSA), Stryker was able to hire what was unquestionably the most talented group of photographers ever brought together on a single project.

Today their names read like a photographic hall of fame. They include such giants of the medium as Dorothea Lange and Walker Evans. They also include Ben Shahn, already regarded as one of the nation's greatest artists; Gordon Parks, destined to achieve fame in several fields of endeavor; and Arthur Rothstein, who would produce some of the most compelling images in the entire collection of approximately two hundred thousand photographs and negatives. Joining them was Russell Lee, the workhorse of the team; Jack Delano; John Vachon; and Carl

Mydans, who, before the project was over, would become known for his very special photographic talent; and Marion Post Wolcott, regarded by many as the hidden star of this extraordinary array of photographers. Arthur Rothstein described this assembled pool of talent as "all working together, under common leadership for a common goal, but . . . [maintaining] completely different and individual styles of photography." Rothstein was also quick to point out that the participants felt a missionary sort of dedication to the FSA project, the desire to produce photographs that would better the lives of so many in need. Along with these regular contributors, other photographers who captured images for the FSA included Edwin Rosskam, Marjory Collins, and Esther Bubley.

From 1935 to 1937 under the name Resettlement Administration and from 1937 to 1942 under the new name Farm Security Administration, Roy Stryker developed the Historical Section into arguably the most efficient and productive section of any federal agency in the nation, sending his photographers into every area of the United States. Their stated goal was to take pictures of FSA agents providing aid to farmers. But he was also in complete agreement with the notion later articulated by historian Irving Bernstein that "the anguish of the American people during hard times demanded a pictorial record." He realized that most of all, such an array of photographic talent, combined with government support, presented a unique opportunity to capture an unprecedented portrayal of a people and a nation, or what he called "a visual encyclopedia of American life."

From the beginning, Stryker instructed his photographers to do far more than take pictures of FSA agents at work. Ultimately, in fact, he destroyed almost all of those types of images. Instead, he told them that their mission was to take photographs that collectively "introduced America to Americans." Later, Stryker would declare that what he was most proud of was the way his photographers were able to "record on film as much of America as we could in terms of people and the land. We photographed destitute migrants and average American townspeople, share-croppers and prosperous farmers, eroded land and fertile land, human misery and human elation." When the project ended, one of Stryker's proudest boasts was that, in his opinion, there wasn't a single picture that portrayed a person in a derogatory manner.

There is no question that this enormous accomplishment would not have been possible

without Stryker's inspired leadership. Before sending the photographers out into the field, where they would remain for significant lengths of time, he would hand them "shooting scripts" that he had prepared. "I'd tell the photographers," Stryker later recalled, "[to] look for the significant detail. The kinds of things that a scholar a hundred years from now is going to wonder about. A butter churn. A horse trough. Crank-handle telephones. Front porches. The horse and buggy. The milk pails and the cream separators. Symbols of the time."

Stryker also demanded that the photographers do considerable homework on their own. His insistence that they go out armed with the facts is perhaps best illustrated by a story he told involving Carl Mydans. "I remember," Stryker stated, "one time when things were pretty bad down in the South and I assigned Carl to do a story about cotton. He had his bags packed and was going out the door and I said to him, 'I assume you know something about cotton.' He said, 'No, not very much.' I called in my secretary and said, 'Cancel Carl's reservation. He's going to stay here with me for a while.' We sat down and we talked almost all day about cotton. We went to lunch and we went to dinner and we talked well into the night about cotton. I told him about cotton as an agricultural product, cotton as a commercial product, the history of cotton in the South, what cotton did to the history of the country, and how it affected areas outside the country. By the time we were through, Carl was ready to go off and photograph cotton."

Several years later, when Mydans had gone on to become a photographer for *Life* magazine, and one of the most important of all the World War II photographers, he wrote, "No one ever worked for him for any length of time without carrying some of Roy Stryker with him. . . . In all the years since I left him, when making pictures I often hear him say, 'Now what are you doing that for? Why are you making that picture?' I still feel I have to justify myself before him as I did when I worked for him."

Stryker left no doubt that as far as FSA's Historical Section was concerned, he was completely in charge. But he was also dealing with some of the most creative and talented photographers, who were hardly the type to take only the pictures that Stryker suggested they take. To his credit, Stryker understood this and quickly recognized how important it was that the FSA file (he never

called it a collection) contain both pictures suggested or dictated by him and pictures taken on the photographers' own initiative. "The Farm Security file," Arthur Rothstein would later state, "would never have been created if we hadn't the freedom to photograph anything, anywhere in the United States—anything that we came across that seemed interesting and vital." Ben Shahn put it simply: "We just took pictures that cried out to be taken." "What we ended up with," Stryker would later declare, "was as well-rounded a picture of American life during that period as anyone could get. The pictures that were used [by magazines and newspapers] were mostly pictures of the Dust Bowl and migrants and half-starved cattle. But probably half of the file contained positive pictures—country square dances and people listening to those big old radios, a soda jerk flipping a scoop of ice cream through the air, the mantel with the family portraits and the old Victorian clock, the nickel hamburger joints and the ten-cent barbershops." The historian Lawrence W. Levine has noted that as a result of having achieved this balance, the FSA photographers "succeeded in creating a remarkable portrait of their countrymen's resiliency and culture . . . a complex blend of despair and faith, despondency and self-sufficiency."

This "remarkable portrait" was made even more extraordinary by a groundbreaking development: the ability to take pictures in full color. By the early 1930, several processes had been introduced, but none was really satisfactory. Then, in 1935, the Eastman Kodak Company introduced a color film called Kodachrome. The pictures it produced were so superior to anything that had previously appeared that it immediately made all other processes obsolete.

It was a most fortunate coincidence that the introduction of viable color photography came at the same time that the FSA photographers began to hit their stride. And although the number of color pictures that Russell Lee, Marion Post Wolcott, Jack Delano, and John Vachon, in particular,

took in color (about sixteen hundred) pales in comparison with what Stryker's team captured in black and white, they represent a most important addition to the file. And for a reason far more meaningful than the physical appeal of color imagery. As the photographic historian Andy Grundberg has written, "The FSA color pictures . . . show an exemplary early use of color as information rather than decoration. . . . The critical and historical importance of [these images] hinges on [their] pioneering use of color as an aid in documenting the subject."

The compilation of the FSA photographic file was unquestionably a remarkable achievement. But in 1941 a major change took place. As it became increasingly likely that the United States would become involved in World War II, and with the FSA increasingly under pressure from Congress to justify its existence, the Historical Section was transferred out of the FSA and into the Office of War Information. At first, Stryker tried to generate enthusiasm for himself and among his photographers for taking pictures documenting the building of the nation's armaments and troops. But as it became apparent that both he and his team were rapidly losing interest in taking pictures of this type of activity, Stryker decided to resign and accept a position as the head of a photography project about to be launched by the Standard Oil Company.

He was not, however, about to embark on his new venture before making one final enormous contribution to future generations and to the world of photography. At this point, there was great uncertainty as to what would happen to the almost two hundred thousand photographs and negatives that made up the FSA file. Some members of Congress opposed almost everything President Roosevelt did and saw little merit in the FSA project; if they had had their way, the photographs would have been destroyed. But Stryker was determined to make sure the file was preserved. Fortunately, it was at this time that his friend the acclaimed writer and poet Archibald MacLeish became head of the Library of Congress. Stryker had always believed that the "nation's library" was the logical place for the FSA photographs to reside. So did MacLeish. Thanks to these two men, in 1944 the FSA photographs and their negatives became a permanent part of the Library of Congress's holdings, now easily accessible via the Internet for all to see and appreciate.

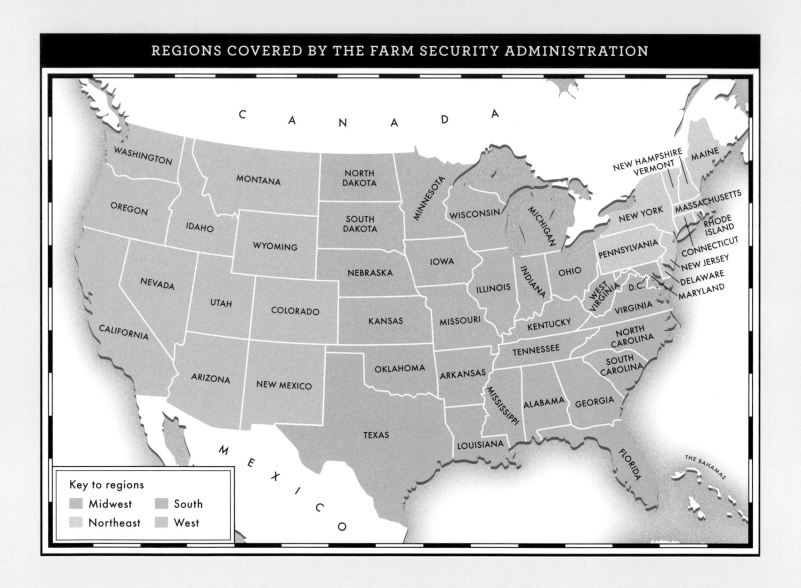

REGIONS COVERED BY THE FARM SECURITY ADMINISTRATION

Key to regions
Midwest
Northeast
South
West

A Regional Approach

———✦———

IN PREPARING A presentation he was about to make to Congress, Roy Stryker wrote, "The task has been to confront the people with each other, the urban with the rural, the inhabitants of one section with those of other sections of the country, in order to promote a wider and more sympathetic understanding of one for the other.... The variety of photographs assembled has been almost as wide as that of life itself. They have come in from the North, South, East and West."

For the FSA photographers, taking pictures in the diverse regions was a life-changing experience. Describing Rothstein's contributions to the FSA, the journalist George Packer wrote, "Think about the strangeness of a New York boy ... sent by the federal government to the hollows of Appalachia to take pictures of terribly poor ... isolated people who were about to be picked up and moved into newly built houses, away from their old homes forever. And to take pictures—and why? In order to have a record of a certain way of life just before it ceased to exist."

This goal of compiling a visual record of "a certain way of life just before it ceased to exist" was vigorously and successfully pursued in every section of the United States and is why this book has been organized by regions.

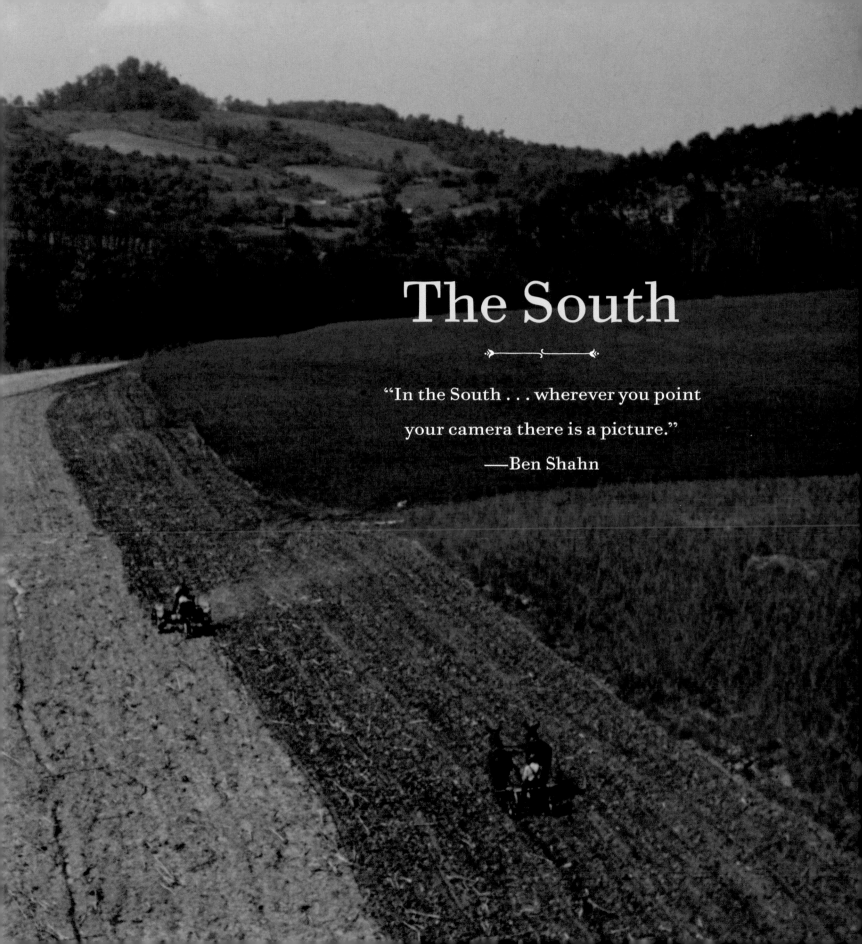

The South

"In the South . . . wherever you point
your camera there is a picture."
—Ben Shahn

AT THE TIME the FSA photographs were taken, the South was, by far, the poorest region in the nation. Millions of people lived on the edge of subsistence, meaning that they had barely enough money for their most basic needs. Among the hardest hit were tenant farmers and sharecroppers, who worked land they did not own. (Sharecroppers divided what they grew with the owners of the property they farmed, while tenant farmers paid their rent in cash.)

For these 8.5 million tenant farmers and sharecroppers, 3 million of whom were African Americans living under the strictures of racial segregation, the coming of the Great Depression reinforced their dreadful situation. As one Black Southerner expressed it, "Most blacks did not even know the Great Depression had come. They had always been poor and only thought the whites were catching up."

The FSA had been established to bring aid to the rural poor, and it was Roy Stryker's mission to document the effects of the Depression. He sent more FSA photographers to the South than into any other region, resulting in more photographs being taken there than in any other section of the country. It was in the South that Walker Evans would earn a reputation as one of the world's greatest photographers. It was in the South that Dorothea Lange would enhance her reputation as a "humanitarian with a camera." It was there that Gordon Parks would

Arthur Rothstein was particularly eager to capture aspects of the American scene before they disappeared. This photograph shows residents of Nethers, Virginia, shortly before the town was abandoned and its residents were relocated.

first use his camera as a weapon against racism, and it was in the South that Marion Post Wolcott would reveal herself as a major photographic talent.

Despite all they encountered, the FSA photographers would produce pictures that depicted the deprivation being felt around the country but that also revealed hope and courage. This idea was perhaps best exemplified by Roy Stryker's assessment of many of Russell Lee's images. "When his photographs would come in," Stryker stated, "I always felt that Russell was saying, 'Now here is a fellow who is having a hard time but with a little help he's going to be all right.'" Later, Stryker would put it more succinctly. "Dignity versus despair," he would state. "I believe that dignity wins out."

Through photographs like this one of Mississippi Delta children, Dorothea Lange became known as a "humanitarian with a camera."

★ 16 ★

"The odds were against them," stated Roy Stryker. "Yet their goodness and strength survived."

WHEN YOU DRINK A
Dr. Pep
GOOD FOR
A BITE TO
COLORED · ADM.
10¢
WHITE MEN ONLY
CASH-NITE FRIDAY
$400.00

A man climbs the stairs to the "colored entrance" of a movie house in Belzoni, Mississippi. Marion Post Wolcott's picture not only is a powerful statement about the racial inequalities of the time, but it also reveals her mastery of light and shadow and composition, basic ingredients of every great photograph.

"[Walker] Evans is the world's greatest expert at photographing empty rooms in houses and making them echo with the people who live there."

—*Life* magazine

Interior of a cabin in Hale County, Alabama. This photograph was one of the many Walker Evans pictures that appeared in Let Us Now Praise Famous Men by Evans and the author James Agee, one of the earliest books that used photography to provide a historical record.

GORDON PARKS was motivated by his belief that "the camera could

be a weapon against poverty, against racism, against all sorts of social

wrongs. . . ." It was in Washington, DC, that he took his best-known

photograph, a portrait of an African American cleaning woman named

Ella Watson. Parks titled the photograph *American Gothic*, the same

title that artist Grant Wood had, twelve years earlier, given his famous

painting of a prim farm couple, regarded by many as a tribute to the

solid nature of white American family life. In Wood's painting, the man

holds a pitchfork, a recognizable symbol of rural America. In Parks's

photograph, the woman in her work dress holds the tools of her trade;

a broom in one hand and a well-used mop in the other, while posed

against an American flag, representing Parks's clear commentary on the

inequities that existed in the United States in 1942.

By portraying Ella Watson with a broom and a mop, Gordon Parks was emphasizing the fact that when
African Americans did find employment, it was almost always confined to menial tasks.

Carl Mydans spoke for many of his fellow photographers when he stated, "I always had the feeling that something good was going to happen in front of me and I wanted my camera to be there." Here, in a photograph by Marion Post Wolcott, a couple jitterbugs in a juke joint outside Clarksdale, Mississippi.

IN JUNE 1938, Dorothea Lange took a photograph of the wife of a migratory laborer named Nettie Featherston that, along with her *Migrant Mother* picture and Arthur Rothstein's photograph of a father and his two sons walking in a dust storm, became an iconic image of the Great Depression era. The photograph's title, *Woman of the Plains*, came from a larger caption in which Lange recorded a conversation she had with Featherston.

"We made good money pullin' [cotton] when we could pull," Featherston said. "But we've had no work since March. . . . The worst thing we did was when we sold the car, but we had to sell it to eat, and now we can't get away from here. We'd like to starve if it hadn't been for what my sister . . . sent me. When it snowed last April we had to burn beans to keep warm. You can't get no relief here until you've lived here a year. This country's a hard country. They won't help bury you here. If you die, you're dead, that's all."

Featherston lived until the age of eighty-one, and she clearly recalled the times in the 1930s when she and her family picked cotton fourteen hours a day. And although her memory of Lange taking pictures of her was hazy, she said that her son remembered the encounter because "the lady gave him two nickels to keep, and his daddy gave him a little tobacco sack to put 'em in. He was so proud."

Lange's photograph of Nettie Featherston, a mother of three and the wife of a migratory laborer, became a classic image of the Depression era.

The purpose of the FSA photographs, John Vachon stated, "should be the honest presentation and preservation of the American scene." Vachon's concern with social justice is evident in his photographic portrayal of African Americans. In this image of Mrs. Louise Dyson, the wife of an FSA borrower and the mother of fifteen children, he made certain that she was surrounded by some of her favorite objects, including an old clock and a religious painting.

HOE CULTURE

Dorothea Lange coined the phrase "hoe culture" in the title for this photograph. Her fellow photographers adopted it.

Dorothea Lange titled this photograph Hoe Culture in the South. *"I'd like to photograph you," she'd say to a subject. They might pose a little, but she would walk around until they forgot about her. Then she would begin to take her pictures.*

In a photograph that [Jack] Delano took during a trip through Georgia . . . four women and a man drag hoes over a mustard-colored field. . . . There is a studied, painterly quality to the strong diagonals of the hoes in contrast to the relaxed bodies moving in the opposite direction. . . . We can almost hear the hoe blades dropping into the rows, and bare feet stamping into the ground. Everything seems to be moving in a harmonious ballet." — author Esmeralda Santiago

Chopping cotton near White Plains, Georgia. "It is my lifelong concern for the common people and appreciation of their value," stated Jack Delano, "that have been the driving force behind everything I have done."

Carl Mydans was not as famous as Dorothea Lange or Walker Evans, but as the Times of London wrote, "One picture, of a Tennessee family living in a hut on an abandoned truck chassis, portrays the misery of the times as starkly as any photographs by his more celebrated contemporaries."

*Perhaps more than any other
FSA photographer, Marion
Post Wolcott was determined
to show the extraordinary
differences in lifestyle between
the disadvantaged and the
advantaged. These people were
luxuriating beside a pool in
Miami, Florida.*

Russell Lee captured this image of the exterior of a workman's family home in Corpus Christi, Texas.

CHILDREN OF THE SOUTH

"I was given freedom to—well, document America." —Marion Post Wolcott

These boys, photographed by Marion Post Wolcott, were fishing in a bayou in Schriever, Louisiana

"It was a really tough time and when this thing came along and this idea that I must wander around the country a bit for three months. . . . I went and I found things that were very startling to me." ——Ben Shahn

Cotton pickers, Pulaski County, Arkansas. Like his fellow FSA photographers, Ben Shahn was struck by the youth of so many of those who labored in the fields of the South.

"There is one thing the photograph must contain," stated photographer Robert Frank, "the humanity of the moment." Russell Lee captured this image of children taking a bath in a community camp in Oklahoma City, Oklahoma.

Throughout the Depression era, southern families were on the move, seeking ways to make a living. Jack Delano photographed these Florida migrants from Shawboro, North Carolina, as they prepared to travel to Cranberry, New Jersey, to pick potatoes.

Sons of day laborers in camp near Webbers Falls, Oklahoma. According to the caption that Russell Lee wrote for this photograph, none of these children had ever attended school.

"In Arkansas I saw a family and they were so miserable that it was unbelievable. The child was holding some ragged doll and the child looked as horribly ragged as the doll. It was an unbelievable situation." —Ben Shahn

Ben Shahn took this compelling photograph of children in the Ozark Mountains. "You can look at a picture for a week . . . and never think of it again," stated the artist Joan Miró. "You can also look at a picture for a second and think of it all your life."

Tree stumps serve as seats in this Scottsville, Alabama, school scene by Carl Mydans.

Right: This photograph by Dorothea Lange shows the daughter of a Randolph County, North Carolina, tenant farmer churning butter.

Opposite: A girl poses for Jack Delano beside her parents' sign in Salisbury, Maryland.

"Photography takes an instant out of time, altering life by holding it still."

—Dorothea Lange

FACES OF THE SOUTH

"It was the first time Americans saw each other's faces and witnessed what life was like across the nation: north to south, east to west, rich and poor, black and white. Ordinary people. Extraordinary times."

—WXXI Public Broadcasting

Photograph by Jack Delano

Opposite: In Little Rock, Arkansas, Dorothea Lange's young subjects wave at her and her camera.

The Midwest

"An editor of *Look* once called [John Vachon] 'our poet
photographer.' That still seems about right."

—*American Heritage* magazine

WHEN THE FSA was formed, the Midwest was widely referred to as "America's Heartland," known for its enormously fertile Great Plains, which had become the "breadbasket of the nation," and for its patchwork of large commercial cities and small towns. Once Roy Stryker had fully assembled his photographic team and sent several of its members into the Midwest, much of the region had turned into what became known as the Dust Bowl.

It is difficult to assign a precise regional location to the Dust Bowl. While the vast area most affected by the disaster cut a swath through the middle of the country, two states in the South, Oklahoma and Texas, were among the hardest hit. Both Dorothea Lange and Russell Lee captured powerful Dust Bowl images, but it was Arthur Rothstein's photographs of a land turned to dust and its human victims that comprised the vivid and unforgettable record of a unique and tragic time in the nation's history.

It was in the Midwest that Ben Shahn, who was already a successful artist, had his photographic awakening, moving from using photographs as subjects for his paintings to becoming a master photographer in his own right. In particular, he excelled at portraying and bringing to life small-town America. It was also in the Midwest that John Vachon discovered his own photographic "voice," enabling him to produce the first in-depth photographic portrayal of an American community. And in the far northern reaches of the Midwest, in North and South Dakota, FSA photographers discovered a topography and way of life much different from anything they had ever encountered, let alone recorded.

Opposite: Jack Delano was particularly skilled at capturing light in all its various forms. He took this photograph in the waiting room of Chicago's Union Station.

"Once in a great while, a photographer comes along whose work . . . really represents what existed in front of the camera with very little intrusion by the photographer. Russell Lee's work has often had this quality."

—photographic historian F. Jack Hurley

Russell Lee captured this image of members of a Pentecostal church in Chicago enraptured in their worship.

At no time . . . did any photographer try to be cute, to ridicule, to take advantage, to in any way show anything but respect for the person he was photographing." —Roy Stryker

On his visit to the nearly abandoned town of Grassy Butte, North Dakota, Arthur Rothstein took this picture of a man who had been forced to close down his store. Rothstein titled the image Waiting for Better Times.

"We tried to present the ordinary in an extraordinary manner." —Ben Shahn

Perhaps because of his long success as an artist, Ben Shahn was a true master at capturing shades of light and dark in his photographs. This father and son were waiting for relief supplies in Urbana, Ohio.

"One morning I photographed a grain elevator: pure sun-brushed silo columns of cement rising from behind a CB&Q freight car. The genius of Walker Evans and [artist] Charles Sheeler welded into one supreme photographic statement, I told myself. Then it occurred to me that it was I who was looking at that grain elevator. For the past year I had been [imitating] the masters. And in Omaha I realized that I had developed my own style with the camera. I knew that [from then on] I would photograph only what pleased me or astonished my eye, and only in the way I saw it." —John Vachon

Freight car and grain elevator, Omaha, Nebraska. The dramatic contrast between the vertical lines of the elevator and the horizontal lines of the freight car made this John Vachon photograph one of the most acclaimed of the FSA images.

"You're having a tough time here and the rest of the country needs to see pictures of it so they can appreciate what you're going through."

——Russell Lee

Dorothea Lange's caption for this picture reads "Dust Bowl farm. Coldwater District, north of Dalhart, Texas. This house is occupied; most of the houses in the district have been abandoned."

"It was in Cimarron County, in the middle of the Oklahoma Panhandle, that I found one of the farmers still on his land. A single cow stood forlornly facing away from the wind in a dusty field. The buildings, barns and sheds were almost buried by drifts and in some places only the tops of the fenceposts could be seen. I decided to photograph this scene.

While making my pictures I could hardly breathe because the dust was everywhere. It was so heavy in the air that the land and sky seemed to merge until there was no horizon. . . .

Just as I was about to stop shooting, I saw the farmer and his two sons walk across the fields. As they pressed into the wind, the smallest child walked a few steps behind, his hands covering his eyes to protect them from the dust. I caught the three of them as they neared the shed." ——Arthur Rothstein

Farmer and sons walking in the face of a dust storm. "Photography," wrote Arthur Rothstein, "is truly a universal language, transcending all boundaries of race, politics and nationality."

Saturday afternoon on Main Street in London, Ohio. "I was primarily interested in people," Ben Shahn declared, "so that I did nothing photographically in the sense of doing buildings for their own sake or a still life or anything like that."

Along Main Street in Lancaster, Ohio. "[Ben] Shahn," wrote the journalist Timothy Egan, "looked for something universal when he pointed his little Leica.... One would ... call [his pictures] what we call all good art: timeless."

Roy Stryker firmly believed that it was in the small towns that the heart of America was most

The A-B-C BARBER SHOP

CHILDRENS
HAIR CUT

AIRCUT   SHAVE

LADIES HAIR
BBING

RE-ELECT
HOPKINS
SHERIFF

Elect The
BETTER SCHOOLS
GROUP

DR. F. O. BECK
WALTER A. NIELSEN
LAWRENCE F. WELCH
N. P. DODGE, JR.
RICHARD E. ROBINSON

ELECT THESE MEN
TO THE SCHOOL BOARD

UNIVERSITY of OMA
FOOTBALL

SCHEDULE
1938

MAKE
Cornhusker
RESERVATIONS NOW!

JAMES T.
ENGLISH
DEMOCRAT
COUNTY ATTORNEY

In this John Vachon photograph, a barber stands in front of his South Omaha, Nebraska, shop. "It's one thing," the photographer Paul Caponigro has stated, "to make pictures of

"One becomes keenly alive to the seeking of picture material," John Vachon wrote. *He captured this image of Omaha citizens as they were watching a parade.*

John Vachon took his Omaha photographs at a time when, in a world where there was no television, photograph-dominated magazines were becoming extremely popular.

Russell Lee's photograph of a pie-eating contest at a 4-H club fair in Cimarron, Kansas. The first 4-H clubs and fairs appeared in the United States as early as 1902.

Opposite: Easter Sunday morning, Chicago, Illinois. Russell Lee set out to photograph as many young people as he could in every section of the country.

"Early on, I found out that it was important to get pictures of the interior of the homes because that showed how people lived, what they ate, the furniture they had."

—Russell Lee

Above: Russell Lee captured this image of a sharecropper's son combing his hair in a shack on a southeastern Missouri farm. Unable to afford wallpaper, many families in rural America used newspapers to cover their walls.

Left: Because photographic lighting equipment was still primitive, many photographers in the 1930s did not take indoor pictures. Russell Lee, however, lugged his bulky camera equipped with giant flashbulbs inside homes to capture images he felt were important.

"If you are the kind of [person] who likes to say 'Am I my brother's keeper?,' don't look at these pictures—they may change your mind."

—photographer Edward Steichen

During the Depression, certain areas of the country were particularly hard-hit. These youngsters,

In this Russell Lee picture, children play in front of a saloon in Gemmell, Minnesota. Roy Stryker instructed his photographers to capture whatever signs they could in their photographs so that future generations could discover what products were popular at the time.

Farm children were forced to be inventive in creating activities away from their chores. Russell Lee took this picture of Williams County, North Dakota, youngsters playing on a homemade merry-go-round.

John Vachon captured this image of a father waiting to lead his children across a downtown Chicago street.

"I have always believed that the American people have the ability to endure. And that is in those faces."

—Roy Stryker

Photograph by Russell Lee

Photograph by

Russell Lee

The West

"[Russell Lee] had an unquenchable curiosity about the life of the country and an affection for ordinary people going about their routines."
—author Nicholas Lemann

"I'M GOING WEST because this country's through," exclaimed one resident of the Dust Bowl. "There isn't anything here for anyone." The story of the American West during the Great Depression is in greatest measure the story of the more than 2.5 million men, women, and children who left the stricken Dust Bowl area and headed for the West, hoping to find work in the fields and orchards of California, Oregon, New Mexico, and the other western states. These migrants presented a tragic spectacle: proud farm families, once the backbone of America, strung out across the highways in their battered "jalopies" that broke down with alarming frequency. Many of the migrants would never reach the West, but of those who did, many discovered that there was little or no work to be found.

Fortunately, there was a photographer who was determined to record what was happening so that the rest of the country and future generations would be aware of what took place during the greatest migration in the nation's history: Dorothea Lange, who, between 1935 and 1939 in an extraordinarily tireless effort, took thousands of photographs of the exodus. The images that she captured would become memorable symbols of the Great Depression. Her contribution was eloquently summarized by the photographic

Opposite: Dorothea Lange's caption for this photograph reads: "Oklahoma sharecropper and family entering California. Stalled on the desert near Indio, California."

historian Robert J. Doherty, who wrote, "This small, shy . . . woman had a strong sense of justice which sparked a silent fury that came to light in the strong emotion of her photographs. With a camera in her hand, she became a giant."

Russell Lee also traveled the length and breadth of the western region. In the midst of his travels, Lee heard of a settlement called Pie Town in a remote area of New Mexico. He was intrigued that it was inhabited by Dust Bowl refugees from Oklahoma and West Texas and that it had gotten its name from one of its original settlers who had baked and sold pies to passersby in the area. Making his way to Pie Town, Lee took a series of photographs depicting families intent on establishing a permanent, self-reliant community after being driven out of their original homes by natural forces. Lee's photographic essay of Pie Town is one of the FSA photographers' greatest demonstrations of how pictures can tell a story without words.

Opposite: Drought refugees from Abilene, Texas, following the crops in California. The father of the family told Dorothea Lange, "I got two brothers still trying to make it back [in Texas] and they're [just] sitting.

"They looked very woebegone to me. . . . I looked at the license plate on the car and it was Oklahoma. I got out of the car, and . . . asked . . . which way they were going. . . , And they said, 'We've been blown out.' . . . They were the first arrivals that I saw. . . . All of that day, I saw these people. And I couldn't wait. I photographed it." ——Dorothea Lange

Refugees from Oklahoma broken down on a highway near Lordsburg, New Mexico. "I am trying to say something about the despised, the defeated, the alienated. . . . About the last ditch," declared Dorothea Lange.

"It's a very difficult thing to be exposed to the new and strange worlds that you know nothing about and find your way. . . . It's a hard thing to be lost."

—Dorothea Lange

Dorothea Lange took this photograph of three motherless children in the migrant camp in which they were living. Young as they were, they worked long hours every day in a California cotton field.

"Their roots were all torn out. The only background they had was a background of utter poverty. It's very hard to photograph a proud man against a background like that, because it doesn't show what he's proud about." —Dorothea Lange

Camped in the rain, three migrant families with fourteen children huddle behind a billboard with a most ironic message. Dorothea Lange took this picture on US Route 99 near Famoso, California.

Lange's caption for this photograph that she took near Calipatria, California, reads: "Living conditions for migratory children in private auto camp during pea harvest. Tent space fifty cents a week."

Young cotton picker, Kern County, California, migrant camp. Dorothea Lange was particularly moved by the plight of the children as she visited migrant camps throughout the West.

"I saw and approached the hungry and desperate mother, as if drawn by a magnet. I do not remember how I explained my presence or my camera to her, but I do remember she asked me no questions. . . . She told me her age, that she was thirty-two. She said that they had been living on frozen vegetables from the surrounding fields, and birds that the children killed. She had just sold the tires from her car to buy food. There she sat in that lean-to tent with her children huddled around her, and seemed to know that my pictures might help her, and so she helped me. There was a sort of equality about it." —Dorothea Lange

This photograph, which Dorothea Lange titled Migrant Mother, has become both the iconic image of the Great Depression and arguably the most reproduced photograph in the history of photography.

"'You were turned loose in a region, and the assignment was more like this: 'See what is really there. What does it look like, what does it feel like? What actually is the human condition?'"

—Dorothea Lange

Marion Post Wolcott took this picture of cowhand Lyman Brewster at a rodeo in Ashland, Montana.

Russell Lee photographed in every region of the country. He captured this image of a couple resting after watching a Fourth of July parade in Vale, Oregon.

A Delta County, Colorado, farmer hauls crates of peaches from his orchard to his shipping shed.
Russell Lee was one of the first of the FSA photographers to take pictures in color.

It is part of the photographer's job to see more intensely than most people do. He must have and keep in him something of the receptiveness of the child who looks at the world for the first time or the traveler who enters a strange country."

—photographer Bill Brandt

PIE TOWN

In this photograph, one of many that Russell Lee took in Pie Town, New Mexico, members of that unique community gather for a "community sing."

Saying grace before a barbecue dinner in Pie Town, New Mexico.
Russell Lee took most of his Pie Town pictures in color.

"[Russell] Lee simply was not comfortable as a photographer showing his subjects as victims. . . . They always seem to have hope."

—author Nicholas Lemann

These are women of the American soil. They are a hardy stock. They are the roots of our country. . . . They are not our well-advertised women of beauty and fashion. . . . These women represent a different mode of life. They are of *themselves* a very great American style. They live with courage and purpose, a part of our tradition."

—Dorothea Lange

An Oklahoma drought refugee photographed in California by Dorothea Lange. "This is a hard way to serve the Lord," she told the photographer.

ALFA NITRATE FILM

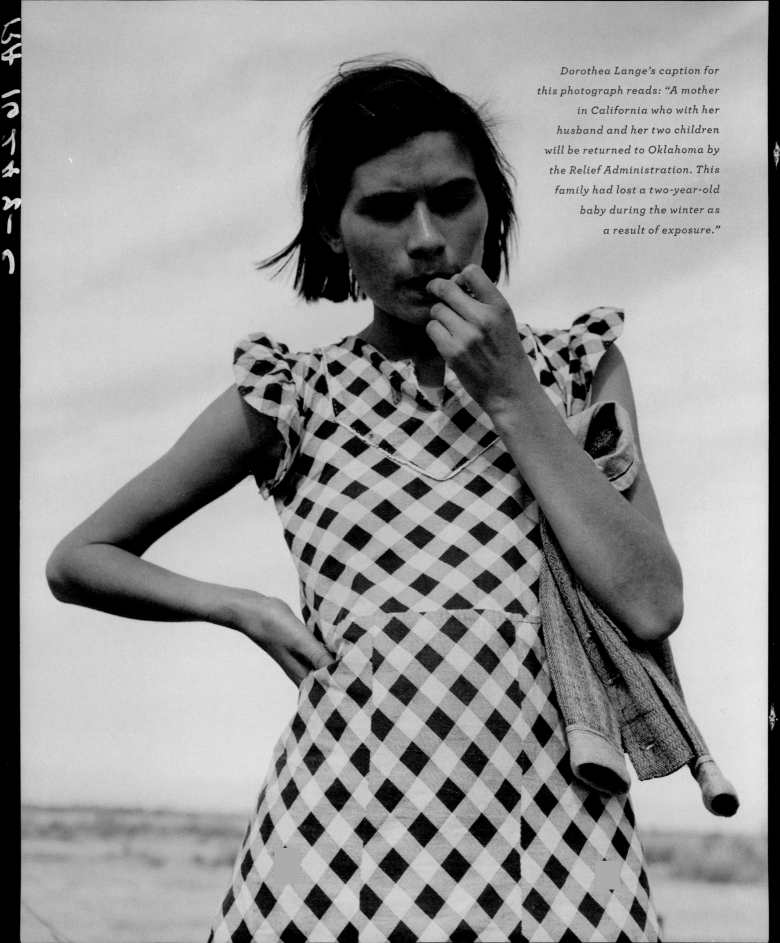

Dorothea Lange's caption for this photograph reads: "A mother in California who with her husband and her two children will be returned to Oklahoma by the Relief Administration. This family had lost a two-year-old baby during the winter as a result of exposure."

Photograph by Dorothea Lange

"Well, I many times encountered courage, real courage. Undeniable courage. I've heard it said that it was the highest quality of the human animal. . . . I encountered that many times, in unexpected places. And I have learned to recognize it when I see it." ——Dorothea Lange

"You could look at the people and see . . . a determination that not even the Depression could kill. The photographers saw it—documented it." —Roy Stryker

Photographs by
Dorothea Lange

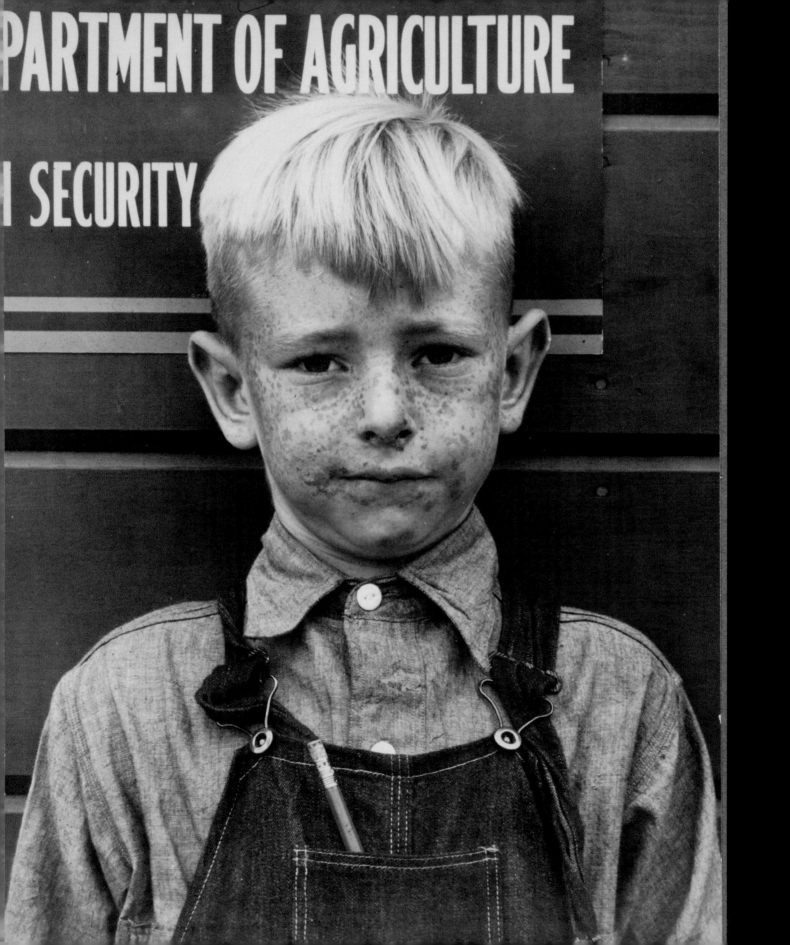

Photograph by Russell Lee

The Northeast

"Through these travels and the photographs
I got to love the United States more than I could
have in any other way." —Jack Delano

THE FSA PHOTOGRAPHY team is best known for its photographs of rural life in the South, for its images of the Dust Bowl that covered the Great Plains of the Midwest, and for its pictures of migrants struggling to find new opportunities in the West. As a number of Roy Stryker's memos and shooting scripts reveal, there was a time when he was concerned that certain parts of the Northeast were being ignored. Soon after sending Marion Post Wolcott into the region, he wrote to her, saying, "By all means take the necessary time that you are going to need to do a good job. It is, after all, terribly important. It is our first chance to do real good winter scenes, and New England has pretty much been neglected, as far as our files are concerned." Wolcott would respond to this letter by capturing an image of the center of Woodstock, Vermont, after a snowstorm, which ranks among the most photographically beautiful images in the FSA file.

Walker Evans explained an important aspect of his photographic approach by stating, "I'm not interested in people in the portrait sense, in the individual sense. I'm interested in people as part of the pictures and as themselves but anonymous." It is an approach that can clearly be seen in the photograph Evans titled *Apartment Buildings,*

Opposite: Along with capturing images revealing the blatant racism of the day, Gordon Parks also took as many photographs portraying African Americans in a positive light as he could. This photo is of a newsboy in the Harlem neighborhood of New York City.

315 and 317 East Sixty-First Street (page 123), a masterly image of New York City in which a solitary man can be seen but is not the most important element in the photograph.

Of all the FSA photographers who captured images throughout the Northeast, none was more productive than Jack Delano. Just as the Midwest would be the place where John Vachon would find his "photographic voice," the Northeast was the site of a great awakening for Delano. "I felt that I was learning," he wrote. "When I would go to cover a county fair, for example; well, I didn't know much about county fairs. . . . [My wife] Irene and I would sit down and work out shooting scripts after going the first day. . . . Not only what was displayed at the fair and all the products . . . but the people and what they wore, and how they looked, and what kind of tobacco they used, and the kids, and the language. . . . And I was studying. I was learning from this and documenting everything I possibly could." Included in the scenes Delano documented was the picture he took of the Windsor Locks, Connecticut, tobacco-raising couple, (page 112), one of the most delightful of all the FSA photographs.

Coal miner Merritt Bundy in his mine on his farm near Penfield, Pennsylvania. "When my father looked at a person," Jack Delano's son told an interviewer, "it was one soul communicating with another."

"So far as I'm concerned, the kind of photography I did in the FSA was . . . based on passionate concern for the human condition." —Jack Delano

"The Lymans were working in their tobacco barn when I came upon them. After chatting for a while about the problems of growing tobacco, I asked them to let me take a photograph of them. At first, Mrs. Lyman demurred. With a giggle, she said, 'Not in this dress. Let me change my clothes.' But after a bit of flattery, she agreed to pose with her husband, just as she was. There they stood, posing stiffly for the photographer, staring morosely at the camera, not at all like the jolly people they really were. So I said, 'Mr. Lyman, I think your pants are falling down.' The peals of laughter that followed were just what I wanted, because *that* was what they were really like." ——Jack Delano

Mr. and Mrs. Andrew Lyman, tobacco farmers near Windsor Locks, Connecticut. "No other photographer,"
a reviewer wrote, "can show the living spirit of the people more clearly than Jack Delano."

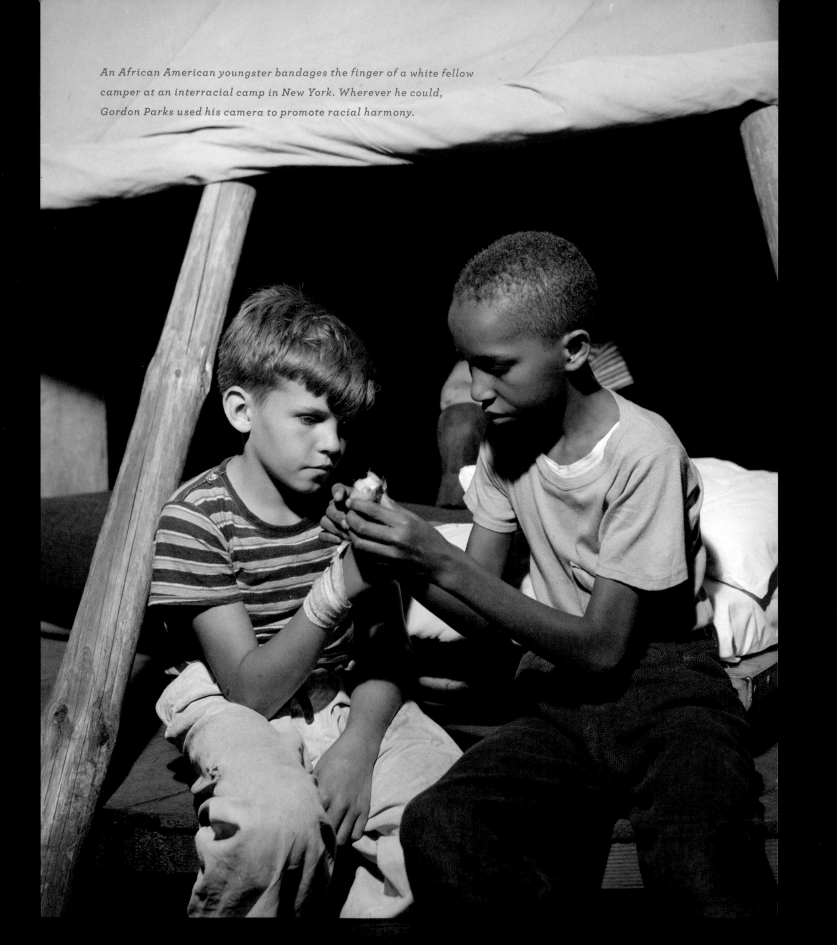

An African American youngster bandages the finger of a white fellow camper at an interracial camp in New York. Wherever he could, Gordon Parks used his camera to promote racial harmony.

"One is not really a photographer until . . . the camera in his hands is an extension of himself. There is where creativity begins."
—Carl Mydans

Two women gossiping at the Albany, Vermont, fair. Carl Mydans's caption for the picture reads: "Things saved for many a day are confided at the fair."

A church steeple, an American flag, a woman rocking peacefully on her front porch. This John Vachon photograph, titled Fourth of July Afternoon, Dover, Delaware, *reveals his determination to include as many upbeat pictures as he could in his FSA images.*

[Photographer Paul Strand said] that to produce an honest photograph, the photographer had to have a 'real respect for the thing in front of him.' The word 'respect' became the guiding principle of everything I was to do in the future. And 'the thing in front of me' became the basic reason for taking a photograph."

—Jack Delano

Jack Delano captured this image at the Vermont State Fair. Like Russell Lee and Marion Post Wolcott, Delano was intrigued by the potential of color photography.

"The small town emerged as a thing possessing [many] advantages: kinship with nature and the seasons, neighborliness, kindness." —Roy Stryker

"I am often reminded of the remark attributed to Abraham Lincoln: 'God must have loved the common people: he made so many of them.'" —Jack Delano

Above: The Peter V. Andrews family in Falmouth, Massachusetts. According to Jack Delano's caption, this Portuguese American family, who received financial assistance from the FSA, had just bought their first cow, which they were very proud about.

Opposite: Although he had been born in Russia and had spent most of his life in New York, Jack Delano developed a great fondness for small-town New England. He titled this photograph Burning the Autumn Leaves *in Norwich, Connecticut.*

"This type of photography . . . was a recognition of the photograph as an art form. This particular project made it quite clear to everybody that photographs have the same value and artistic qualities as good drawings, as paintings, as pieces of sculpture; that they can be examples of fine art." —Arthur Rothstein

Arthur Rothstein would become best known for the manner in which he was able to capture the harsh realities of the Dust Bowl. But in photographs like this one of a Vermont dairy barn, he demonstrated that he could also produce images that could stand on their own as works of art.

Roy Stryker asked his photographers to take pictures of the aftermath of snowstorms. No one accomplished this more

The rebel of the FSA photography team, Walker Evans, who took this now-famous photograph of a Bethlehem, Pennsylvania, cemetery and steel mill, declared, "I did a whole lot of things on my own. . . . I just used . . . to go

Best known for her photographs of Americans caught up in hard times, Dorothea Lange took this picture depicting the other end of the spectrum. Her caption for this photograph of a wealthy woman in New York City reads: "Some New Yorkers use personally owned limousines driven by private uniformed drivers."

CHILDREN OF THE NORTHEAST

"I was not surprised by Roy [Stryker's] request for some 'positive images.' . . .
To tell the truth, I often took pictures of that sort without any urging from Roy,
simply because that was part of the America I saw." —Jack Delano

"I always had the feeling . . . that something was going to happen in front of me, and when it did I wanted my camera to be there." ——Carl Mydans

The American Legion, an organization made up of US war veterans, was founded in 1919. While photographing in Bethlehem, Pennsylvania, Walker Evans captured this image of sons of Legion members about to take part in one of the organization's events.

Responding to Roy Stryker's request for photographs of people engaged in activities linked to the Northeast, Arthur Rothstein took this picture of cranberry pickers in Burlington County, New Jersey. Three-fourths of the workers in the picture are children.

Gathering sap for making maple syrup. In her caption for this picture, Marion Post Wolcott wrote: "Sugaring is a social event and is enjoyed by all the young people and children in the neighborhood."

Children playing in New York City. Although he traveled the country taking photographs for the FSA, Arthur Rothstein, who was born, raised, and educated in New York City, often returned home to photograph scenes with which he was especially familiar.

"The faces to me were the most significant part of the file."

——Roy Stryker

Photograph by Carl Mydans

Photograph by Gordon Parks

Photograph by
Walker Evans

Right: Photograph by Jack Delano

Opposite: Photograph by
Arthur Rothstein

An Extraordinary Achievement

ROY STRYKER BELIEVED that the most important part of his job was to make sure that the FSA photographs were seen by as many people as possible, including government officials at every level. From the beginning, he made it clear that any magazine or other publication could use the FSA pictures free of charge. As a result, and given the content of the photographs and their extraordinary quality, the images filled the pages of *Life, Look, Fortune,* and scores of other magazines—so much so that, in a report to the government, FSA staff members boasted that they were supplying magazines around the world with an average of fourteen hundred photographs a month.

Many books combining FSA photographs with text were also published. Among the most acclaimed were *Land of the Free* by Archibald MacLeish, *Home Town* by Sherwood Anderson, *Twelve Million Black Voices* by Richard Wright, *An American Exodus* by Dorothea Lange and Paul Taylor, *American Photographs* by Walker Evans, and *Let Us Now Praise Famous Men* by Walker Evans and James Agee. In a world that had previously not considered photographs as art, this collection of images became the subject of major exhibitions in some of the nation's largest and most prestigious museums—a testament to the quality and impact of the art form.

One of the immediate results of the photographs' being so widely seen was that local and national government officials, shocked by what many of the images revealed, began to take action. In California, for example, the federal government started erecting migrant camps with running water, toilet facilities, and other necessities to house the hordes of displaced migrants who had found themselves in an even more desperate situation once they reached the West Coast. Photographs taken by Rothstein, Lee, and Lange compelled Congress to pass relief bills aimed at supplying financial aid to Dust Bowl victims. At the same time, thanks to Lee's pictures of miners and mining, Congress also initiated and eventually enacted the nation's first mine-safety laws. Commenting on what she regarded as one of the most important results of the images that she and her fellow FSA photographers captured, Marion Post Wolcott declared, "I feel that the FSA [and the photographs we took were] . . . the beginning of . . . governmental assumption of responsibility for the individual."

And there was much more. As the photographic historians Gilles Mora and Beverly W. Brannan have observed, "[The FSA photographs] became an important means through which the nation came to comprehend its own vastness and diversity." That was an outcome in keeping with Stryker's and his photographers' greatest mission—capturing on film as much of America and American life as possible.

They certainly did that. And in the process, they had a gigantic effect not only on the nation's comprehension of itself but also on the history and nature of the medium in which they worked. Toward the end of his FSA career, Roy Stryker recalled that "in 1936 photography, which theretofore had been mostly a matter of landscapes and snapshots and family portraits, was fast being discovered as a serious tool of communication, a new way for a thoughtful, creative person to make a statement." No single group of photographers has ever done that more consistently or more powerfully than the FSA photographer corps.

The Roosevelt administration committed billions of dollars to building roads, bridges, and other structures to put people back to work and to various relief programs to help the victims of the Great Depression. But what still shapes our image of this remarkable era are the photographs taken by Stryker's team—Delano, Evans, Lange, Lee, Mydans, Parks, Rothstein, Shahn, Vachon, and Wolcott.

Given what the FSA photographic team accomplished, it is only natural to wonder why such a project has never been repeated. It's not a newly-posed question. According to the author George Packer, in the 1970s Arthur Rothstein publicly wondered why every twenty-five years, photographers couldn't go out again and create "a record of what the United States is like, what life is like in the United States."

Attempting to answer this intriguing question, Packer stated that for such a project to be undertaken again, "immensely talented and economically desperate men and women had to [be] willing to spend months and years traveling around the country's hardest places. . . . A government had to be in place that wanted to record those places and people before they disappeared and to spend the money doing it." For both of these reasons, Packer concluded, "it's unlikely that America will have such a mirror held up to its face again."

Almost ninety years after the sweeping endeavor led by Roy Stryker and undertaken by his talented team, the photographs gathered in the FSA collection represent a unique accomplishment. They played a pivotal role in establishing documentary photography as a major creative field of art. And, almost a century on, the images still go right to our hearts, reflecting a varied portrait of America and its people as they lived through a time of great hardship.

Profiles

------◆------

JACK DELANO

Jack Delano was born in Ukraine in 1914 and moved to New York with his family in 1923. While studying music at the Pennsylvania Academy of the Fine Arts, he was awarded a fellowship to travel in Europe. It was there that he bought his first camera and fell in love with photography. When Delano returned to the United States, he submitted samples of the pictures he had taken to Roy Stryker, who gave him a job as an FSA photographer.

His hiring not only gave him much-needed employment; it also provided him the opportunity to pursue a deep-rooted desire—to celebrate the common people, a passion that shows through in almost every photograph he took for the FSA. Gilles Mora and Beverly Brannan expanded on this notion when they wrote, "Much of Delano's work was informed by an interest in people who performed necessary but thankless work; he approached the subject as a fine artist, searching for the quintessential image to convey the dignity of their labor. Roy Stryker referred to this sensibility when he recalled Delano's effort to capture the essence of Vermont in a simple photo while his colleagues tried to document as many scenes and activities as they could."

Delano's fortunes took both a personal and professional turn when Stryker assigned him to photograph conditions in Puerto Rico. There he produced some of his most heartfelt photographs—and also fell in love with the island and its people.

When Roy Stryker left the FSA to direct a photographic project for the Standard Oil Company, Delano went with him as a staff photographer. He soon gave in to his heart's desire and moved to Puerto Rico, where he first produced films for Puerto Rico's Division of Community Education and then became a director of the government's television service. At the same time, he and his wife, Irene, wrote and designed books for children. Jack Delano died in 1997.

WALKER EVANS

Born in St. Louis, Missouri, in 1903, Walker Evans spent hours as a child taking snapshots of his family and his friends with a small Kodak camera. After a year at Williams College, he left school and moved to New York City, where he worked in bookstores and at the New York Public Library. In 1927, after writing essays and short stories in Paris, he returned to New York, intending to become a writer. However, he also rediscovered the camera and soon decided that photography provided him his best avenue of expression. What no one could have anticipated was that he possessed a talent resulting in a body of photographic work that would lead the legendary photography critic Lincoln Kirstein to ask, "What poet has said as much? What painter has shown as much?"

By the time Roy Stryker hired him to join his photographic corps, Evans had already earned a reputation as one of the most gifted young photographers in the nation through photographs that had appeared in the book *The Bridge* by the famous author Hart Crane and a series of widely seen

pictures that he had taken in 1933 of street life in Cuba. Thanks in great measure to the images he captured for the FSA, he would eventually be regarded by many as the best documentary photographer of the twentieth century. Yet, as Stryker quickly discovered, Evans was also extremely temperamental and would produce fewer photographs than any of his colleagues. As much as Stryker admired Evans's work, he eventually felt it necessary to let Evans go. But the hundreds of photographs Evans took include many of the most popular and acclaimed images in the file.

Like most of his fellow Historical Section photographers, Evans experienced a highly productive post-FSA life. In 1938, the Museum of Modern Art in New York mounted a major showing of his work in the first one-person photographic exhibition ever held. The museum also published Evans's book *American Photographs*, regarded by one of today's reviewers as "the benchmark against which all photographic monographs are judged." In 1945, Evans became a staff photographer and eventually director of photography at *Fortune* magazine. When he left that publication in 1965, he was appointed professor of photography at Yale University. In 1971, the Museum of Modern Art mounted another retrospective of his work. Walker Evans died in 1975.

"You put your camera around your neck in the morning along with putting on your shoes," proclaimed Dorothea Lange, "and there it is, an appendage of the body that shares your life with you." Like Walker Evans, Lange came to the FSA having already earned a reputation as a topflight photographer. Lange was born in Hoboken, New Jersey, in 1895. She began her career as a portrait photographer, first in New York City and then in San Francisco. When the Great Depression hit, she gave up her portrait taking and took her camera to the streets, where she photographed San Franciscans who had lost their jobs. Her powerful and sensitive images of the unemployed and homeless would earn her the title "humanitarian with a camera." They also caught the attention of Roy Stryker, who invited her to join the FSA photographers corps.

The hundreds of photographs that Lange took for the FSA—of migrant families on the road and arriving in California, looking for work in the fruit and vegetable fields; of life in the migrant camps; and of the hard-hit yet proud migrants—became the most published and best known in the entire FSA file. Her photograph titled *Migrant Mother* remains one of the most famous and most reproduced photographs in the world.

Lange photographed for the FSA for more than four years, crisscrossing the nation, documenting the plight and courage of dispossessed families, capturing her images with a special motive in mind. "It was her intention," said one of her close friends, "to motivate change with every picture she took."

Shortly after World War II began, Lange was hired by the War Relocation Authority to photograph the internment of more than 120,000 Japanese Americans during the conflict. Her photographs were so powerful and so critical of the unjust imprisonment that the government kept them hidden from the public for some thirty years. In 1945, she began to teach photography at the California School of Fine Arts. Seven years later, Lange cofounded *Aperture*, a magazine that would become one of the most important photography publications in the world. In Lange's late years, she received numerous awards, and many publications celebrated her and her body of work. She died in San Francisco in 1965.

RUSSELL LEE

Russell Lee has been called "the man who made America's portrait." He was born to wealthy parents in Ottawa, Illinois, in 1903. After earning a degree in chemical engineering, he spent six years studying painting before discovering and developing a passion for photography. While he was involved in painting, he met Ben Shahn, who recommended him to Roy Stryker. The director developed an instant liking to Lee, but he had no idea that he was about to hire the man who would become the most prolific photographer in his corps, the man who would spend weeks at a time in a particular locale, whether it be a remote

agricultural town or an urban center like Chicago or New York, capturing more than twenty-three thousand images.

Lee was tireless, and he had two great advantages—a wife who traveled with him and saw to it that he maintained his schedule, and an inherited personal fortune that eased the cares that most of his colleagues had on the road. He had enormous sensitivity and talent, particularly in his ability to portray his subjects not as victims or as people who had been defeated by large devastating social forces, but as people who always seemed to have hope that things would get better. Perhaps that is why, even though Dorothea Lange and Walker Evans are far more famous photographers, reproductions of Lee's photographs have been more frequently requested on the Library of Congress's website than those of any other FSA photographer.

After almost six years of photographing for the FSA, Lee joined Stryker on the ambitious Standard Oil project. He then became a freelance photographer for almost every major magazine in the nation. In 1965 he found a whole new calling and a whole new love when he became a professor of photography at the University of Texas at Austin. Lee died in 1986.

CARL MYDANS

Born and raised in Boston, Carl Mydans spent almost his entire life involved in photojournalism. After graduating from Boston University's school of journalism, he began his career as a freelance reporter for the *Boston Globe* and the *Boston Post*, followed by a brief stint as a staff writer for *American Banker*. In 1931, he acquired a 35mm camera and entered the world of photojournalism. As New York's International Center of Photography has noted, "Mydans was now able to translate into the visual what was sometimes difficult to describe with words alone."

In 1935, Mydans's photographs grabbed the attention of Roy Stryker, who hired him as one of the earliest members of the FSA photography team. Mydans's first assignment was to take pictures of the cotton industry in the South. The images he captured there demonstrate not only his mastery of light, shadow, and composition but also his special ability to photograph with compassion

the dispossessed and exploited men, women, and children who lived and toiled there.

Mydans's time with the agency was brief (only sixteen months), but he was able to photograph for the FSA in other areas of the country as well. In 1936, he became one of *Life* magazine's first photographers and remained with that publication for thirty-six years. His greatest fame came with World War II, when he distinguished himself as one of the world's most accomplished combat photographers. His photographs, seen by millions, include the famous image of General Douglas MacArthur wading ashore in the Philippines, signaling the virtual end of the fighting in the South Pacific.

Mydans's work for *Life* continued after the war and included four years spent as chief of the Time-Life news bureau in Tokyo and a return to combat photography during the Korean War. He also carried out photographic assignments for *Time*, *Fortune*, and *Smithsonian* magazines. The author of several books, Carl Mydans died in 2004.

GORDON PARKS

Gordon Parks was a true Renaissance man, rising from the depths of poverty and racial prejudice to succeed as a photographer, movie director, musician, composer, writer, and artist. He was born on November 30, 1912, in Fort Scott, Kansas. His mother died when he was fifteen, and he was sent to live with relatives but soon found himself on the street. Over the next two decades, he was forced to take a variety of jobs to support himself, including waiter, ticket collector, janitor, singer and piano player, and railway porter. It was during this period that a specific incident changed the direction of his life. While working as a porter, he picked up a magazine that a passenger had left behind and was moved almost to tears by a spread of photographs taken by FSA photographers about migrant workers. "From that moment," he would later write, "I was determined to become a photographer. Three days later I bought my first camera at a pawnshop for $7.50.... I had bought what was to become my weapon against poverty and racism."

Now living in Chicago, Parks began taking photographs and submitting them to newspapers and magazines. His photographs of the city's African American population, focusing on the ills of poverty and racism, brought him a highly prestigious Julius Rosenwald Fellowship, which captured the attention of Roy Stryker. Knowing the huge risk he would be taking in hiring a photographer with so little experience, an African American certain to encounter the same racial prejudice suffered by those he would be photographing, Stryker nonetheless invited Parks to Washington and made him a member of his photography team. Parks responded by producing images both powerful and sensitive, including the iconic photograph of the African American cleaning woman Ella Watson holding a broom and a mop against a backdrop of the American flag, symbolizing the African American struggle against racism.

In the years after the FSA was disbanded, Parks demonstrated his amazing versatility in a number of ways. He became *Life* and *Vogue*'s first Black photographer. Not only did he make important contributions to the fields of ballet and opera, but he also became the first African

American to write, direct, and compose the music for a Hollywood film. The man who never finished high school received forty honorary doctorates and awards, including the National Medal of Arts. Gordon Parks died in 2006.

ARTHUR ROTHSTEIN

Born in 1915, Arthur Rothstein grew up in the Bronx in New York City and became interested in photography at an early age. While attending Columbia University, he met Roy Stryker and carried out several photographic assignments for him. He was the first photographer to be hired when the Historical Section of what became the Farm Security Administration was formed.

For Rothstein, working with the FSA was a life-changing experience. "I was a provincial New Yorker," he would later say. "It was a wonderful opportunity to travel around the country and see what the rest of the United States was like. Also, there was a kind of feeling of great excitement in

Washington in those days, the feeling you were in on something new and exciting, a missionary sense of dedication to this project, of making the world a better place in which to live."

During his five years with the photographers corps, Rothstein contributed some fourteen thousand images to the FSA file. Among them are many of the most memorable. He will, however, undoubtedly be best remembered for his 1936 series of photographs of the Dust Bowl and its victims. Among them is the image titled *Father and sons walking in the face of a dust storm*, which, along with Dorothea Lange's *Migrant Mother*, remains one of the two most iconic images of the Great Depression.

Along with his photographs, Rothstein made other important contributions to the FSA project, including setting up its first darkroom. And it was he who recognized the immense importance of captioning an image. "A photographer," he stated, "must be aware of and concerned about the words that accompany a picture. These words should be considered as carefully as the lighting, exposure and composition of the photograph."

From 1941 to 1946, Rothstein worked for the Office of War Information and then for the US Army Signal Corps in Asia. In 1947, he became a photographer for *Look* magazine and later served as its director of photography, until the publication ceased operations in 1971. He also taught photojournalism at his alma mater, Columbia University, was head of photography for *Parade* magazine, and was the author of the book *Photojournalism: Pictures for Magazines and Newspapers*. Arthur Rothstein died in 1985.

BEN SHAHN

Born in Kaunas, Lithuania, in 1898, Ben Shahn came to America with his family in 1906. In the 1920s, he studied art at New York's National Academy of Design and then traveled throughout Europe, where he became familiar with the work of both classical and contemporary European artists. Returning to New York, he captured the attention of the art world through his paintings and murals, including a series of murals he created with the Mexican artist Diego Rivera.

In New York, Shahn shared a studio with Walker Evans, who was a great admirer of the powerful way in which Shahn often conveyed the theme of social justice in his art. Despite his growing fame in the art world, Shahn was in need of steady employment. Evans recommended him to Roy Stryker, who hired Shahn to create posters and other artwork promoting the FSA project, but he also handed him a camera and told him to experiment with it. "I put a Leica in his hands," Stryker later recounted, "and said, 'Go out and fool around with it.' [He] came back with pictures that were like his paintings—imaginative, beautiful things not restricted by technique." Stryker wasted no time in changing Shahn's FSA status from creator of promotional materials to photographer.

During his time with the FSA, Shahn photographed mostly in the South and the Midwest. It was in the South on his first assignment that he made an important personal discovery. Unlike Evans, who regarded photographs as works of art, Shahn initially thought of photographs as sketches that would later help him paint the scene before him. However, once he saw the results of his picture taking in the South, he became convinced that his photographs could be regarded as art in and of themselves.

In 1941, Shahn shocked Stryker and his fellow FSA photographers by suddenly announcing that he had decided to give up photography. He spent much of World War II creating posters for the Office of War Information. After the war, his popularity rose to new heights as he became recognized as one of the world's greatest artists. The recipient of the highest honors the art world had to bestow, he spent the last twenty years of his life delivering lectures at universities and other venues around the world. He also became a professor at Harvard University and wrote several books, including the influential *Biography of a Painting* and *The Shape of Content*. Shahn died in 1969.

ROY STRYKER

Roy Stryker was born in 1893 in Great Bend, Indiana, and grew up on a farm in Montrose, Colorado. After serving in the army in World War I, he received a degree from Columbia University and remained there to teach economics. Intrigued by photography, he regularly used images to illustrate his lectures, a practice that served as excellent preparation for his leadership role in compiling the FSA photographic collection. When his work with the FSA was nearing completion, Stryker worked for Standard Oil of New Jersey (SONJ) on a project to use photography to improve the company's public image. He began his work on that project by persuading Russell Lee and Gordon Parks to join him. He then filled out his camera corps

by hiring future legends of the medium Berenice Abbott, Todd Webb, and Elliott Erwitt.

From 1943 to 1950, the SONJ photographers took some 67,000 pictures, making it the "largest documentation project ever undertaken in America by anyone other than the federal government." Stryker then directed the establishment of a photographic library to document life in the city of Pittsburgh. In 1952, he conducted seminars in photojournalism at the University of Missouri before he retired.

Stryker died in Grand Junction, Colorado, in 1975. Since his death, historians and photographic experts from around the world have heaped praise on the man directly responsible for the success of the FSA project, many of them commenting on how Stryker transformed the way people look at photographs. Perhaps the most incisive comment came from the photography historian F. Jack Hurley, who said it was Roy Stryker's inspired leadership that enabled the FSA photographers to teach the world that "a photograph could be beautiful and still possess a social conscience."

JOHN VACHON

In 1936, at a time when millions of his fellow Americans were out of work, John Vachon "lucked into" a job in the FSA's Historical Section. "My job," he recalled, "was to write captions in pencil onto the back of 8 x 10 glossy prints of photographs. I would copy out such identifications as Dust Storm, Cimarron Co. Okla. . . . new house of tenant farm family, etc. And then I would . . . stamp on

the back . . . photo by Arthur Rothstein. Or it might say Ben Shahn, Dorothea Lange, Walker Evans, Carl Mydans. I had never heard of any of these names."

He may never have heard of them, but during the times that he and Walker Evans were in the FSA offices together, he impressed the already-acclaimed photographer with his personality and his obvious desire to better himself. As the two became friendly, Evans taught Vachon how to use an 8 x 10 view camera. On his own, Vachon began to practice taking pictures with a small 35mm Leica and was soon capturing images all around Washington. When Roy Stryker saw what his caption writer had produced, he hired him as a full-fledged member of the FSA photographic team.

It was a wise decision. Vachon not only produced images of the highest quality, but he also continually demonstrated his clear understanding of what Stryker and his fellow FSA photographers believed was their main purpose. "We are today," he stated, "making a conscious effort to . . . leave for the future a very living document of our age, of what people today look like, of what they do." When Stryker left the FSA to direct photography projects for the Standard Oil Company of New Jersey, Vachon went with him as a staff photographer. In 1947, he began a more than twenty-five-year stint as one of *Look* magazine's most important photographers. John Vachon died in 1975 at the age of sixty.

MARION POST WOLCOTT

Born in Montclair, New Jersey, in 1910, Marion Post Wolcott began her career as a teacher in a small town in Massachusetts. When the school closed in 1932, she traveled to Europe, where she met the accomplished photographer Trude Fleischmann, who encouraged Wolcott's budding attempts at photography and urged her to pursue it as a profession. Returning to the United States, she carried out freelance photography assignments for several magazines, including *Life* and *Fortune*, before landing a position as a staff photographer for the *Philadelphia Evening Bulletin*. In 1938, her friend the photographer Paul Strand recommended Wolcott to Roy Stryker, who invited her to join his photographers corps.

As a woman traveling great distances, Wolcott faced enormous challenges. Unlike Dorothea Lange, whose husband accompanied her on many of her assignments, Wolcott traveled alone at a time when it was regarded as improper for a woman to do so. It was also dangerous for a woman to be traveling alone, especially at night and in extremely remote areas. But, accompanied by Stryker's constant written advice on how she should dress and behave, she persevered and photographed from Vermont to Mississippi and from Kentucky to Montana, capturing images so sensitive and of such high quality that today she is regarded by many photography experts as one of the most talented of the FSA photographers.

Unlike all of Stryker's other photographers, Wolcott had no post-FSA photography career. In 1941, she met and married a man and devoted her life to raising a family. Her extraordinary body of work is punctuated by this recollection of what the FSA photography project was all about: "We were all inspired and revved up by the . . . idea . . . of . . . trying to get people to understand what was going on, and what the condition of the country was. We were trying to show this graphically, because people will look at photographs when they won't read things. We hoped that this would make an impact and change people's ideas and their opinions."

Source Notes

An Extraordinary Time

p. 3: "There are two things . . . had to be appreciated": quoted in Sandler, *America Through the Lens*, 68.

p. 4: "all working together . . . styles of photography": quoted in Cohen, xviii.

p. 4: "the anguish of . . . a pictorial record": Fleischhauer and Brannan, 27.

p. 4: "a visual encyclopedia of American life": quoted in "Introducing America to Americans: Depression-Era Photographs from the Museum of Fine Arts, Houston," Pearl Fincher Museum of Fine Arts, https://www.pearlmfa.org/exh17-introducing-america-to-americans.html.

p. 4: "introduced America to Americans": quoted in Fleischhauer and Brannan, 40.

p. 4: "record on film . . . human elation": ibid.

p. 4: "there is not a single photograph . . . derogatory manner": ibid.

p. 6: "I'd tell the photographers . . . Symbols of the time": quoted in Nancy Wood, "In This Proud Land," *American Heritage*, August 1973, https://www.americanheritage.com/proud-land.

p. 6: "I remember . . . photograph cotton": quoted in Stryker, 13.

p. 6: "No one ever . . . worked for him": quoted in Hurley, *Portrait of a Decade*, 175.

p. 7: "The Farm Security . . . interesting and vital": quoted in Fleischhauer and Brannan, 10.

p. 7: "We just took pictures . . . to be taken": quoted by Timothy Egan in the introduction to Shahn, xiii.

pp. 7–8: "What we ended . . . ten-cent barbershops": quoted in Nancy Wood, "In This Proud Land," *American Heritage*, August 1973, https://www.americanheritage.com/proud-land.

p. 8: "succeeded in creating . . . self-sufficiency": Fleischhauer and Brannan, 27.

p. 9: "the FSA color . . . documenting the subject": quoted in *Bound for Glory*, 10.

A Regional Approach

p. 11: "The task has been . . . East and West": quoted in Cohen, 2.

p. 11: "Think about the . . . ceased to exist.": quoted in Rothstein, *Fields of Vision*, 10.

The South

p. 13: "In the South . . . a picture": quoted by Timothy Egan in the introduction to Shahn, xii.

p. 15: "Most blacks . . . were catching up": quoted in Anthony J. Badger, *The New Deal: Depression Years, 1933–1940*, New York: Farrar, Straus & Giroux, 1989, 28.

p. 15: "humanitarian with a camera": quoted in Sandler, *America Through the Lens*, 99.

p. 16: "When his photographs . . . all right": quoted in Fleischhauer and Brannan, 33.

p. 16: "Dignity versus despair . . . dignity wins out": ibid., 36.

p. 17: "The odds were . . . strength survived": ibid.

p. 20: "[Walker] Evans is the world's . . . who live there": Walter McQuade, "Visual Clues to Who We Were, and Are: A Walker Evans Retrospective," *Life*, March 5, 1971.

p. 21: "[Walker] Evans recorded . . . a surgeon": Department of Photographs, "Walker Evans (1903–1975)," *Heilbrunn Timeline of Art History*, Metropolitan Museum of Art, http://www.metmuseum.org/toah/hd/evan/hd_evan.htm.

p. 22: "the camera . . . social wrongs": quoted by Charles Johnson in the introduction to Parks, *Fields of Vision*, x.

p. 27: "I always had the feeling . . . to be there": quoted by Annie Proulx in the introduction to Mydans, ix.

p. 28: "We made good . . . that's all": quoted in Mike Goad, "Nettie Featherston, 1938," *Exit78* (blog), August 30, 2016, https://exit78.com/nettie-featherston-1938/.

p. 28: "the lady gave . . . was so proud": ibid.

p. 30: "should be the honest . . . American scene": quoted in Vachon, *John Vachon's America*, 12.

p. 31: "I'd like to photograph you": quoted in Fleischhauer and Brannan, 115.

p. 32: "In a photograph . . . harmonious ballet": Esmeralda Santiago in the introduction to Delano, *Fields of Vision*, x.

p. 32: "It is my lifelong . . . I have done": quoted in Delano, *Photographic Memories*, 56.

p. 34: "One picture, of . . . celebrated contemporaries": quoted by Annie Proulx in the introduction to Mydans, xi.

p. 38: "I was given freedom . . . America": quoted in Walther, 478.

p. 39: "It was a really tough time . . . startling to me": ibid., 364.

p. 39: "There is one thing . . . of the moment": quoted in Nathan Lyons, ed., *Photographers on Photography: A Critical Anthology*, Englewood Cliff, NJ: Prentice Hall, 1966, 66.

p. 41: "In Arkansas . . . an unbelievable situation": "Oral History Interview with Ben Shahn, April 14, 1964," Archives of American Art, Smithsonian Institution, https://www.aaa.si.edu/collections/interviews/oral-history-interview-ben-shahn-12760#transcript.

p. 41: "You can look . . . all your life": quoted in Dore Ashton, *Twentieth-Century Artists on Art*, New York: Pantheon, 1985, 9

p. 44: "Photography takes . . . holding it still": quoted in "Quotes by Dorothea Lange," American Masters, PBS, August 25, 2014, https://www.pbs.org/wnet/americanmasters/dorothea-lange-quotes-by-dorothea-lange/3159/.

p. 45: "It was the . . . Extraordinary times": "Documenting the Face of America: Roy Stryker and the FSA/OWI Photographers," WXXI, August 20, 2010, https://www.wxxi.org/node/41577.

The Midwest

p. 49: "An editor of . . . . seems about right": Thomas B. Morgan, "John Vachon: A Certain Look," *American Heritage*, February 1989, https://www.americanheritage.com/john-vachon-certain-look.

p. 54: "Once in a . . . this quality": quoted in Hurley, *Portrait of a Decade*, 118.

p. 55: "At no time . . . was photographing": "Oral History Interview with Roy Emerson Stryker, 1963–1965," Archives of American Art, Smithsonian Institution, https://www.aaa.si.edu/collections/interviews/oral-history-interview-roy-emerson-stryker-12480#transcript.

p. 55: "We tried to . . . an extraordinary manner": quoted in Fleischhauer and Brannan, 65.

p. 57: "One morning . . . I saw it": quoted in Walther, 180–181.

p. 58: "You're having a . . . going through": quoted in "Introduction: Russell Lee Photograph Collection," Briscoe Center for American History, University of Texas at Austin, https://www.cah.utexas.edu/feature/lee/book_intro9.php.

p. 58: "Dust Bowl farm . . . have been abandoned": Dorothea Lange, *Dust Bowl farm*, June 1938, Farm Security Administration, Office of War Information Photograph Collection, Library of Congress, https://www.loc.gov/item/2017770620/.

p. 61: "It was in Cimarron . . . the shed": quoted in Hurley, *Portrait of a Decade*, 84.

p. 61: "Photography is truly . . . politics and nationality": quoted in "Avery Architectural and Fine Arts Library Acquires Arthur Rothstein Photographic Collection," Columbia University Libraries, October 16, 2014, https://library.columbia.edu/about/news /libraries/2014 /2014-10-16_Avery_Library_Acquires_Arthur_Rothstein_Collection.html.

p. 62: "Dust is too much . . . Oklahoma": Arthur Rothstein, *Dust is too much for this farmer's son*, April 1936, Farm Security Administration, Office of War Information Photograph Collection, Library of Congress, https://www.loc.gov/item/2017760331/.

p. 63: "If you would like . . . ever seen": Ernie Pyle, *Ernie's America: The Best of Ernie Pyle's 1930's Travel Dispatches*, New York: Random House, 1989, 113.

p. 64: "I was primarily . . . like that": quoted in John A. Benigno, "Ben Shahn," *Masters of Photography* (blog), September 2, 2011, http://mastersofphotography.blogspot.com/2011/09/ben-shahn.html.

p. 64: "[Ben] Shan looked . . . timeless": Timothy Egan in the introduction to Shahn, ix.

p. 66: "It's one thing . . . who they are": quoted in John Paul Caponigro, "21 Quotes by Photographer Paul Caponigro," *John Paul Caponigro* (blog), September 13, 2013, https://www.johnpaulcaponigro.com/blog/12085/21-quotes-by-photographer-paul-caponigro/.

p. 67: "One becomes keenly . . . picture material": quoted in Vachon, *John Vachon's America*, 27.

p. 68: "[Russell Lee's] essential . . . every image": quoted in "Texas Originals: Russell Lee," Humanities Texas, https://www.humanitiestexas .org/programs/tx-originals/list/russell-lee.

p. 70: "Early on . . . furniture they had": quoted in Burt A. Folkart, "Russell Lee, 1930s Photo Artist, Dies," *Los Angeles Times*, August 31, 1986, https://www.latimes.com/archives/la-xpm-1986-08-31-me-15088-story.html.

p. 71: "If you are . . . change your mind": quoted in Fleischhauer and Brannan, 63.

p. 75: "I have always . . . those faces": ibid., 33.

The West

p. 79: "[Russell Lee] . . . about their routines": quoted by Nicholas Lemann in the introduction to Lee, *Fields of Vision*, xii.

p. 81: "I'm going West . . . for anyone": Dorothea Lange, *Man living on "Scratch Hill" outside Atoka, Oklahoma*, June 1938, Farm Security Administration, Office of War Information Photograph Collection, Library of Congress, https://www.loc.gov/resource/fsa.8b38690/.

p. 81: "Oklahoma sharecropper . . . Indio, California": Dorothea Lange, *Oklahoma sharecropper and family entering California. Stalled on the desert near Indio, California,* February 1937, Farm Security Administration, Office of War Information Photograph Collection, Library of Congress, https://www.loc.gov/item/2017769657/.

p. 82: "This small, shy . . . became a giant": quoted in Sandler, *American Image*, 187.

p. 82: "I got two brothers . . . they're [just] sitting": Dorothea Lange, *Drought refugees from Abilene, Texas,* August 1936, Farm Security Administration, Office of War Information Photograph Collection, Library of Congress, https://www.loc.gov/resource/fsa.8b38482/.

p. 84: "They looked . . . I photographed it": "Oral History Interview with Dorothea Lange, May 22, 1964," Archives of American Art, Smithsonian Institution, https://www.aaa.si.edu/collections/interviews/oral-history-interview-dorothea-lange-11757#transcript.

p. 84: "I am trying . . . the last ditch": quoted in River Bullock, "Written by Dorothea Lange," Museum of Modern Art, February 26, 2020, https://www.moma.org/magazine/articles/245.

p. 85: "It's a very difficult . . . to be lost": quoted in Lange, 56.

p. 87: "Their roots were . . . proud about": ibid., 62.

p. 88: "Living conditions . . . fifty cents a week": Dorothea Lange, *Living conditions for migratory children in private auto camp during pea harvest,* February 1939, Farm Security Administration, Office of War Information Photograph Collection, Library of Congress, https://www.loc.gov/resource/fsa.8b33330/.

p. 90: "I saw and approached . . . equality about it": quoted in Lange, 76.

p. 92: "You were turned . . . human condition?": quoted in Elizabeth Partridge, ed., *Dorothea Lange: A Visual Life,* Washington, DC: Smithsonian Institution Press, 1994, 111.

p. 96: "It is part . . . strange country": quoted in John Paul Caponigro, "21 Quotes by Photographer Bill Brandt," *John Paul Caponigro* (blog), April 28, 2014, https://www.johnpaulcaponigro.com/blog/13188/18-quotes-by-photographer-bill-brandt/.

p. 97: "[Russell] Lee was . . . to have hope": quoted by Nicholas Lemann in the introduction to Lee, *Fields of Vision*, xi.

p. 98: "These are women . . . part of our tradition": quoted in Lange, 103.

p. 98: "This is a . . . serve the Lord": Dorothea Lange, *"This is a hard way to serve the Lord." Oklahoma drought refugee, California,* March 1937, Farm Security Administration, Office of War Information Photograph Collection, Library of Congress, https://www.loc.gov/resource/fsa.8b31740/.

p. 99: "A mother in . . . result of exposure": Dorothea Lange, *A mother in California . . . ,* March 1937, Farm Security Administration, Office of War Information Photograph Collection, Library of Congress, https://www.loc.gov/resource/fsa.8b31749/.

p. 100: "Well, I many times . . . I see it": quoted in Lange, 131.

p. 101: "You could look . . . documented it": quoted in Fleischhauer and Brannan, 33.

The Northeast

p. 107: "Through these travels . . . other way": quoted in Taschen, 99.

p. 109: "By all means . . . are concerned": quoted in Mora and Brannan, 38.

p. 109: "I'm not interested . . . but anonymous": "Oral History Interview with Walker Evans, October 13–December 23, 1971," Archives of American Art, Smithsonian Institution, https://www.aaa.si.edu/collections/interviews/oral-history-interview-walker-evans-11721.

p. 110: "I felt that I was learning . . . I possibly could": quoted in Walther, 112.

p. 110: "When my father . . . with another": quoted in Mora and Brannan, 129.

p. 111: "So far as . . . human condition": quoted in Lee, Collier, and Delano.

p. 113: "The Lymans were . . . really like": quoted in Delano, 55.

p. 113: "No other photographer . . . Jack Delano": quoted in Laura Brauer, "Ordinary People: Jack Delano," *Rangefinder*, January 1, 2010, https://www.rangefinderonline.com/news-features/industry-news/ordinary-people-jack-delano/.

p. 115: "One is not . . . creativity begins": Carl Mydans, "In Mind and Heart," *Life*, December 23, 1966.

p. 115: "Things saved . . . at the fair": Carl Mydans, *Things saved for many a day are confided at the fair, Albany, Vermont*, September 1936, Farm Security Administration, Office of War Information Photograph Collection, Library of Congress, https://www.loc.gov/item/2017716252/.

p. 116: "[Photographer Paul Strand said] that . . . a photograph": quoted in Delano, *Photographic Memories*, 25.

p. 118: "The small town emerged . . . neighborliness, kindness": quoted in Fleischhauer and Brannan, 59.

p. 119: "I am often . . . many of them": quoted in Delano, *Photographic Memories*, 56.

p. 120: "This type of photography . . . fine art": "Oral History Interview with Arthur Rothstein, May 25, 1964," Archives of American Art, Smithsonian Institution, https://www.aaa.si.edu/collections/interviews/oral-history-interview-arthur-rothstein-13317.

p. 122: "I did a whole . . . before my eye": quoted in Walther, 324.

p. 123: "In his own . . . a camera": quoted in Hurley, *Portrait of a Decade*, 48.

p. 124: "Some New Yorkers . . . uniformed drivers": Dorothea Lange, *Fifth Avenue approaching 57th Street. New York City*, July 1939, Farm Security Administration, Office of War Information Photograph Collection, Library of Congress, https://www.loc.gov/pictures/item/2017772208/.

p. 125: "What impels me . . . they mean": quoted by Esmerelda Santiago in the introduction to Delano, *Fields of Vision*, viii.

p. 126: "I was not surprised . . . I saw": quoted in Delano, *Photographic Memories*, 59.

p. 127: "I always had the feeling . . . camera to be there": Annie Proulx in the introduction to Mydans, ix.

p. 128: "Sugaring is . . . in the neighborhood": Marion Post Wolcott, *Hired man, young neighbor (Julia Fletcher), collie dog, and Frank H. Shurtleff's son gathering sap from sugar trees for making syrup*, April 1940, Farm Security Administration, Office of War Information Photograph Collection, Library of Congress, https://www.loc.gov/item/2017756261/.

p. 131: "The faces . . . of the file": quoted in Fleischhauer and Brannan, 33.

An Extraordinary Achievement

p. 136: "I feel that . . . the individual": quoted by Francine Prose in the introduction to Wolcott, xii.

p. 136: "[The FSA photographs] . . . and diversity": quoted in Mora and Brannan, 20.

p. 136: "in 1936 photography . . . a statement": quoted in Wroth, 122.

p. 137: "a record . . . the United States": quoted by George Packer in the introduction to Rothstein, *Fields of Vision*, xii.

p. 137: "immensely talented . . . doing it": ibid.

p. 137: "it's unlikely . . . face again": ibid.

Profiles

pp. 139–140: "Much of . . . as they could": quoted in Mora and Brannan, 188.

p. 140: "What poet . . . shown as much?": quoted in "Picturing America," Edwynn Houk Gallery, July 14, 2020, https://www.houkgallery.com /news/143-picturing-america-ilse-bing-walker-evans-dorothea-lange-edward/.

p. 141: "the benchmark against . . . are judged": Department of Photographs, "Walker Evans (1903–1975)," *Heilbrunn Timeline of Art History*, Metropolitan Museum of Art, http://www.metmuseum.org/toah/hd/evan/hd_evan.htm.

p. 142: "You put your . . . your life with you": Lange, vii.

p. 142: "humanitarian with a camera": quoted in Sandler, *America Through the Lens*, 99.

p. 143: "It was her intention . . . she took": ibid., 100.

p. 143: "the man who made America's portrait": Wittliff Gallery of Southwestern & Mexican Photography, *Russell Lee: A Centenary Exhibition*, pamphlet, Spring 2003; San Marcos, Texas.

p. 144: "Mydans was now . . . words alone": International Center of Photography, "Carl Mydans," *Encyclopedia of Photography*, New York: Crown, 1984, 351.

p. 146: "From that moment . . . poverty and racism": quoted by Charles Johnson in the introduction to Parks, *Fields of Vision*, x.

pp. 147–148: "I was a provincial . . . in which to live": "Oral History Interview with Arthur Rothstein, May 25, 1964," Archives of American Art, Smithsonian Institution, https://www.aaa.si.edu/collections/interviews/oral-history-interview-arthur-rothstein-13317.

p. 148: "A photographer must . . . the photograph": quoted in John A. Benigno, "Famous Photography Quotes," *Masters of Photography* (blog), http://mastersofphotography.blogspot.com/p/famous-photography-quotes.html.

p. 149: "I put a Leica . . . by technique": quoted by Timothy Egan in the introduction to Shahn, xi.

p. 150: "largest documentation . . . federal government": quoted in "The Photographers: Roy E. Stryker," http://www.info-ren.org/projects /btul/exhibit/photog14.html.

p. 151: "a photograph . . . social conscience": ibid.

p. 151: "My job was . . . these names": quoted in Vachon, *John Vachon's America*, 3.

p. 152: "We are today . . . what they do": quoted by Kurt Andersen in the introduction to Vachon, *Fields of Vision*, viii.

p. 153: "We were all inspired . . . their opinions": quoted in Linda Wolcott-Moore, "Marion Post Wolcott: Photography for the Farm Security Administration," The Photography of Marion Post Wolcott, http://people.virginia.edu/~ds8s/mpw/mpw-fsa.html.

Bibliography

Appel, Mary Jane. *Russell Lee: A Photographer's Life and Legacy*. New York: Norton, 2020.

Bound for Glory: America in Color 1939–43. Introduction by Paul Hendrickson. Washington, DC: Library of Congress, 2004.

Cohen, Stu. *The Likes of Us: America in the Eyes of the Farm Security Administration*. Boston: Godine, 2009.

Daniel, Pete, et al. *Official Images: New Deal Photography*. Washington, DC: Smithsonian Institution Press, 1987.

Delano, Jack. *Fields of Vision: The Photographs of Jack Delano*. Introduction by Esmerelda Santiago. Washington, DC: Library of Congress, 2010.

———. *Photographic Memories*. Washington, DC: Smithsonian Institution Press, 1997.

Evans, Walker. *American Photographs*. New York: Museum of Modern Art, 1938.

Fleischhauer, Carl, and Beverly W. Brannan, eds. *Documenting America 1935–1943*. Oakland: University of California Press, 1989.

Hurley, F. Jack. *Marion Post Wolcott: A Photographic Journey*. Albuquerque: University of New Mexico Press, 1989.

———. *Portrait of a Decade: Roy Stryker and the Development of Documentary Photography in the Thirties*. Baton Rouge: Louisiana State University Press, 1972.

Lange, Dorothea. *Photographs of a Lifetime*. New York: Aperture, 1982.

Lee, Russell. *Fields of Vision: The Photographs of Russell Lee*. Introduction by Nicholas Lemann. Washington, DC: Library of Congress, 2008.

Lee, Russell, John Collier Jr., and Jack Delano. *Far from Main Street: Three Photographers in Depression-Era New Mexico*. Santa Fe: Museum of New Mexico Press, 1994.

Mora, Gilles, and Beverly Brannan. *FSA: The American Vision*. New York: Abrams, 2006.

Mydans, Carl. *Fields of Vision: The Photographs of Carl Mydans*. Introduction by Annie Proulx. Washington, DC: Library of Congress, 2011.

Parks, Gordon. *A Choice of Weapons*. New York: Harper & Row, 1966.

———. *Fields of Vision: The Photographs of Arthur Rothstein*. Introduction by George Packer. Washington, DC: Library of Congress, 2011.

———. *Fields of Vision: The Photographs of Gordon Parks*. Introduction by Charles Johnson. Washington, DC: Library of Congress, 2011.

Rothstein Arthur. *Arthur Rothstein: Words and Pictures*. New York: AmPhoto, 1979.

Sandler, Martin W. *America Through the Lens: Photographers Who Changed the Nation*. New York: Henry Holt, 2005.

———. *American Image: Photographing One Hundred Fifty Years in the Life of a Nation*, New York: Contemporary Books, 1989.

———. *The Dust Bowl Through the Lens: How Photography Revealed and Helped Remedy a National Disaster*. New York: Bloomsbury, 2009.

———. *Photography: An Illustrated History*. New York: Oxford University Press, 2002.

Shahn, Ben. *Fields of Vision: The Photographs of Ben Shahn*. Introduction by Timothy Egan. Washington, DC: Library of Congress, 2008.

Stryker, Roy Emerson, and Nancy Wood. *In This Proud Land: America, 1935–1943, as Seen in the FSA Photographs*. New York: Galahad, 1973.

Vachon, John. *Fields of Vision: The Photographs of John Vachon*. Introduction by Kurt Andersen. Washington, DC: Library of Congress, 2010.

———. *John Vachon's America: Photographs and Letters from the Depression to World War II*. Edited by Miles Orvell. Berkeley: University of California Press, 2003.

Walther, Peter. *New Deal Photography: USA 1935–1943*. Cologne, Germany: Taschen, 2017.

Wolcott, Marion Post. *Fields of Vision: The Photographs of Marion Post Wolcott*. Introduction by Francine Prose. Washington, DC: Library of Congress, 2008.

Wroth, William, ed. *Russell Lee's FSA Photographs of Chamisal and Peñasco, New Mexico*. Santa Fe: Ancient City Press, 1985.

Photography Credits

All the photographs in this book are courtesy of the Library of Congress. Photographer, title, and year are provided here for uncaptioned images.

p. i: Marion Post Wolcott, *Guests of Sarasota trailer park, Sarasota, Florida, enjoying the sun and sea breeze at the beach*, 1941

pp. iv–1: John Vachon, *Riding the ranch in winter, Lyman County, South Dakota*, 1940.

p. 2: John Vachon, *Lincoln, Nebraska*, 1942

p. 5: Arthur Rothstein, *Housing conditions in Ambridge, Pennsylvania. Home of the American Bridge Company*, 1938

p. 7: Arthur Rothstein, *Girl at Gees Bend*, Alabama, 1937

p. 8: John Vachon, *Farm boys eating ice-cream cones*, Washington, Indiana, 1941

pp. 12–13: Marion Post Wolcott, *Planting corn along a river in Northeastern Tennessee*, 1940

pp. 48–49: John Vachon, *Church near Junction City, Kansas*, 1942

pp. 78–79: Russell Lee, *Filling station and garage at Pie Town*, New Mexico, 1939 pp. 106–107: Jack Delano, *Connecticut town on the sea, probably Stonington*, 1940

pp. 134–135: Jack Delano, *Landscape on the Jackson Farm, vicinity of White Plains*, Georgia, 1941

p. 137: Arthur Rothstein, *Children playing, New York City, New York*, 1941

p. 138: Russell Lee, *Steele, Missouri. A crowd in front of an itinerant photographer's tent*, 1938

p. 139: Photographer unknown, *Jack Delano, Farm Security Administration/Office of War Information photographer, full-length portrait, holding camera, standing on front of locomotive*, c. 1943

p. 141: Edwin Locke, *Walker Evans, profile, hand up to face*, 1937

p. 142: Photographer unknown, *Dorothea Lange, Resettlement Administration photographer, in California*, 1936

p. 143: Photographer unknown, *Portrait of Russell Lee, FSA (Farm Security Administration) photographer*, c. 1942

p. 145: Carl Mydans, *Carl Mydans, Farm Security Administration photographer (self-portrait)*, c. 1935

p. 146: Photographer unknown, *detail from Gordon Parks, Farm Security Administration/Office of War Information photographer, standing in office*, c. 1943

p. 147: Photographer unknown, *Arthur Rothstein, FSA (Farm Security Administration) photographer*, 1938

p. 149: Photographer unknown, *Ben Shahn, Farm Security Administration photographer*, 1938.

p. 150: Russell Lee, *Roy E. Stryker, photograph chief of the U.S. Farm Security Administration, standing in street, probably in Washington, D.C.*, 1938

p. 151: Photographer unknown, *John F. Vachon, Farm Security Administration photographer*, 1942

p. 153: Arthur Rothstein, *Marion Post Wolcott with Zeiss Ikoflex III and Speed Graphic in hand in Montgomery County, Maryland*, 1940

Index

Page numbers in italics indicate a reference to a photograph or caption.